Sanctuary from Stress

Sanctuary from Stress

A Step-by-Step Guide to Creating Sanctuary Wherever You Are

Sherri Reed

Sanctuary from Stress

A Step-by-Step Guide
to Creating Sanctuary
Wherever You Are

Copyright © 2020 by Sherri Reed

ISBN: 978-1-7923234-3-0
ISBN: 1-7923-2343-3
Library of Congress Control Number: 2020911794

Sacred Life Publishers™
SacredLife.com
Printed in the United States of America

Contents

*I would like to dedicate this book to
James Sturdivant.*

*His help and dedication in researching the aspects
of this book has been invaluable.*

*My love and appreciation for his integrity,
intelligence and great sense of humor
is heartfelt!*

It is my intention that this book will guide,
inspire and assist you in the creation
of your personal Sanctuary space.

A space that will nourish your soul and
offer a newfound peace of mind
and a more peaceful life!

Bask in your own creativity.

Blessings for a memorable journey in creating
your own Sanctuary wherever you are.

~ Sherri Reed

Introduction

Creating Sanctuary Wherever You Are is Divinely inspired – literally. It's part of an imperative given to me by a Divine presence during a near-death experience when I was a teenager. At that time, I was told to create sanctuaries in the world— places of rest, recovery, and renewal for those suffering from the unrelenting stresses of modern life, especially those who spend their lives caring for others. I have lived my entire adult life in pursuit of that mission.

My dedication to my mission has led me to create, at different times, six Sanctuary Centers where burned-out caregivers such as healers and ministers came to receive massage, color and aromatherapy, personalized cuisine, prayer, solitude, inspiration and other forms of rejuvenation. It has led me to write this book and share with everyone the revitalizing benefits of creating, and taking refuge in, your own sanctuary. And it has motivated me to create a line of Sanctuary Living products that enable anyone to create Sanctuary wherever they are. In the process, I have developed Sanctuary as a whole lifestyle designed to counteract the life diminishing effects of stress.

Evidence of the need for Sanctuary is all around us. Stress is endemic. How successfully we deal with it determines the quality of our lives. There are many well-known techniques for dealing with stress—but they are all made more effective when performed in a space designed to enhance the stress relief process. Sanctuary is such a place, a sacred space that fills all the senses with relaxation generators, from the soothing stimulation of therapeutic colors to the subtle sounds of nature. Everyone needs Sanctuary!

Creating your own Sanctuary Space is also one of the greatest acts of "self-care". Taking time to take care of self is self-care! Rest, relax, and renew.

I hope that in the following pages you will find not only practical advice for turning virtually any quiet space into Sanctuary but also the inspiration to use Sanctuary to actively enhance your life. For many, Sanctuary is a place to practice self-support and renewal. Guests walk into Sanctuary feeling stressed and walk out feeling refreshed. For others, such as myself, it is a place to experience spiritual inspiration. I encourage everyone to explore the benefits Sanctuary holds for their own lives. It is often a life changing experience.

Sherri Reed
Founder, Sanctuary For Life

*Set peace of mind
as your highest goal,
and organize your life around it.*

~ Brian Tracy

Chapter 1

Called to Care

I grew up like a lot of girls in my part of town; loved, affluent, and sheltered. I went to a church that taught me to be kind, giving, and self-denying. During my school years I had good friends and great times. I was well liked by my classmates, except for a few bullies, and went to fun parties. I had a wonderful life and a bright future. I wanted to help people and be the best wife in the world when I grew up.

Then I went to a party.

I was seventeen. My boyfriend, Richard, invited me to a party at a friend's house and, of course, I said yes. We had a good time. We danced, we talked, and Richard and I shared a drink given to us by a friend. Then he took me home and kissed me goodnight.

The next day, the friend who had given us the drink became ill. People said he just collapsed and was rushed to the hospital. It turned out that he had hepatitis. So, everybody who was at the party with him got a phone call telling us to go get a gamma globulin shot. Richard and I went to the doctor together, but his family didn't have any money and he couldn't afford his shot, so I gave him mine, just as I believed I had been taught to do. When the nurse came in with just one shot and asked which one of us was to get it, I pointed to Richard—and I didn't tell anyone because I didn't want to embarrass him.

Hepatitis is a disease that eats away your liver. The experts say it takes about two weeks for the symptoms to show up, but when you're young and vibrant it can take longer. When I did start feeling symptoms, my entire being mentally, physically, and emotionally was altered. I lost control of my emotions. I couldn't function. Everything was overwhelming. I didn't know what was wrong with me. It was as if my entire life force was draining away. I didn't want to disappoint my parents by being a complainer, so I kept my symptoms to myself, never once thinking I might have a deadly disease.

One day I woke up dizzy and confused. When I tried to walk, I couldn't walk straight. I kept running into the walls. That frightened me terribly. I thought I must be going crazy.

I stumbled into the kitchen and told a family acquaintance, "I feel like I'm dying!" To my surprise that person handed me a knife and said, "Well, then, why don't you just go ahead and kill yourself?" I was shocked and confused. I would never kill myself! However, I found myself staggering and dashing down the street into the woods with a knife in my hand, crying hysterically.

As I was running it was as if my brain split in two and a part of me said, "Stop! What are you doing? Why are you doing this?" And as soon as I stopped running, I turned around and found my brother was there. He had run after me and, when I stopped, he assured me everything was going to be all right, that I was going to be okay. That calmed me down enough to realize that I needed to go home. My brother was the only one who could have done that. I have been grateful to him for that ever since.

When I got back home, I finally noticed the danger signs and told my parents to place me in a mental hospital. Even as a young girl I had always been pretty self-aware, and I knew that what I was doing was not rational. I wasn't thinking clearly; I wasn't able to verbalize clearly—but nobody around me had any idea these were symptoms of hepatitis, most of all me.

After that, I remember being shuffled from one car to another amid the chaos and confusion. My parents were scared and confused as to what was wrong with me. They took me to a compound of buildings cloistered off the road that turned out to be a mental hospital. There were five buildings in a circle and there was a sidewalk around the circle going into each building. All the buildings looked the same except one, and that one gave me a horrifying feeling. By the time we got there, I was mentally paralyzed and mindlessly signed a waiver saying I was committing myself, without knowing what I was doing. I had no idea I had just given the people who ran that place complete power over my body, my mind, and my life. In essence, I had signed my life away. I heard screams and horrible yelling; I was terrified, and I wanted to be anywhere else but there. But it was too late. I was trapped.

Because of the incident with the knife, they decided I was dangerous, gave me pills to calm me down, and put me in the building that gave me a frightening feeling. That was maximum security. It was a sterile, cold, and cruel place. As the drugs took effect, I remember watching everybody around me and thinking, "This isn't happening; this isn't real!" I realized what a mistake I had made, that I wasn't crazy and I wanted out of there! But it was too late. I was locked up. Not even my parents could get in to see me or talk to me.

From then on, I was The Dangerous One. When somebody stole a plastic knife from the lunchroom, they accused me of it, and I found myself thinking I must have done something wrong. That's what their intimidation did to me—it made me doubt myself and wonder if I really was crazy—that, and the disease toxins building up in my body and brain day by day.

After a time, as I lay there shivering, a beautiful young girl who looked like an angel came into my terrorized world, the only pleasant sight I had seen since my arrival. She was a patient like me and she came to my bedside, gently shook me, and said, "Hi, my name is Allyson. Do you want to do something fun? Come on, follow me, I'll take care of you."

So, I got out of bed, put on my slippers, and went down the hall with her to an empty room. There she handed me an old-fashioned, thick glass perfume spray bottle. It smelled old and sweet, almost like my grandmother. She had one, too. Then, unexpectedly, she threw her bottle against the wall. It shattered and she screamed, "Do it! Do it! Do it!" Though I was shocked speechless, I felt like screaming, "My reality's not like yours!" I wanted to run away but, abruptly, alarms went off. I froze and just stood there with that bottle. Allyson took the bottle out of my hand and threw it against the wall. That's when the men in white coats came in and carried both of us away to different places. They thought I had thrown a bottle and treated me horribly after that. I never saw Allyson again.

All the beds at this mental hospital had rings at the foot and at the head. Those were there to strap the patients down for electroshock treatments. It turned out that the hospital was conducting major electroshock therapy at the time. After lunch, I would see the orderlies in their white coats coming down the hall and everyone in the ward would start screaming. When the orderlies came into the room, they picked out one patient and strapped them down to their bed, spread eagle. Then they would wheel the electroshock machine beside the bed, attach the electrodes, and put a rubber stick in their victim's mouth. Then the lights would flicker and, when it was over, the patients went into a deep sleep for about forty-five minutes. After that, the doctors would stimulate them somehow, and the patients would wake up acting like zombies. They would bloat up and walk around not knowing who they were. They couldn't remember the conversation we had the day before. They were fried. I was terrified that was going to happen to me.

Even my parents couldn't reach me in there. They called our family attorney, telling him, "They won't let us see our daughter!" So, one day I escaped! It wasn't easy, but I felt invisible. I went to a building in the middle of the institution where the main office was, broke in, and called my boyfriend. "Please come get me, come get me!" I begged, but then they caught me—and before I knew it, I was in a straitjacket with needles going into me and I was thrown all alone into a room with thick pads on the walls. No one loved anyone in that hospital. If you weren't crazy when you came in, that place would make you crazy.

After I had been in the hospital about three weeks, I reached a point when I just couldn't take it anymore. I staggered into the nurse's quarters and said, "I feel like I'm dying!" They took my temperature. It was 105 degrees. This time they believed me. They still didn't know it was hepatitis because my medical records showed I had received a gamma globulin shot, the shot I had given to my boyfriend. So, they moved me out of maximum security and into a ward that had been evacuated to protect people from this terrible, unknown disease. I was in quarantine. They treated me like I was Typhoid Mary.

Now people were coming at me in special suits with masks and gloves. The way they were treating me told me something was seriously wrong with me—but I could only wonder what it was. They say then I began to drift in and out of consciousness. I don't remember. I just know I must have been in that condition for weeks because there came a point when I could no longer walk.

One day I remember begging for a glass of water, but no one would give me one. The nurse who had been the meanest to me had this terrible look of alarm on her face. They took my temperature and I felt a sudden rush of energy all around me. The next thing I knew, they pulled back my covers and started throwing alcohol all over my naked body. As soon as they did that, time went into slow motion and the aroma of frankincense and myrrh almost overpowered me with a very pungent but very desirable fragrance, the most intense fragrance I had ever smelled. Somehow, I knew this was the essence of Jesus.

The mean nurse knelt at the foot of my bed and started to cry. Flashes of light and darkness swirled around me like a whirlwind: light, darkness, light, darkness, like opposing forces fighting each other. A doctor said, "We're losing her!" and I remember thinking, "You're not losing me! Losing me where?" But I was frozen in my body and could not speak.

The next thing I remember was being lifted out of my body, up into a corner of the room, watching the doctors work on me and shout orders to the nurses. Then, I found myself going through a long tunnel. I passed through the tunnel in super slow motion, with thoughts firing in my mind much faster than I could ever really think. That was because they weren't my thoughts. Those thoughts were being downloaded into me — and they were filled with messages. The process was effortless.

While I was in the tunnel I was told that there would come a time when I was to create five "Sanctuary For Life" centers in various places around the world, where people could come and experience a profound, healing, rejuvenating experience that would change their lives forever. I was also told to show people how to create sanctuary experiences wherever they might be. This, I was told, was to be my mission in life.

At the end of the tunnel was a magnificent White Light. It was so brilliant I wanted to bathe in it, let it absorb me, and embrace it for eternity. But almost as soon as I reached the Light, I was turned back. I remember being disappointed by that but also completely at peace with it. I was told, "It's not your time; you're to go back and help people heal, especially women." It was more of a "knowing" than a "hearing". Then, as soon as I had been turned back, I was back in my body. Even through the pain I felt, I knew something had shifted, something had happened to me. I came back different.

After a time (I don't know how long), I woke up one morning, alone, knowing that something serious had happened but feeling pretty good about it because I was still alive. I had heard them say they lost me, but I was still here. Then I noticed that there were brown paper bags taped up all over the mirror in my room.

It took everything I had to get the covers off my body, and I was wobbly as I stood. There was no one in my room to help me so I had to hold on to the bed and then the dresser to get to the mirror. All those bags just weren't making any sense to me. So, when I got to the mirror, I ripped one of the bags down, saw myself—and screamed. I hadn't seen myself in a mirror since they put me in quarantine and now looking at myself was like seeing a ghost. I had gone from a 128-pound, vibrant seventeen-year-old to a ninety-eight pound creature of skin and bones with no hair and yellow acne. I don't remember what happened after that. All I know is I passed out, and when I woke up, I found myself back in bed.

When I woke up, all the paper sacks were gone. I remembered what had happened earlier as more of a dream than reality. I wondered, "Whoa, did that even happen? You're in a mental hospital after all!" I had to go back to the mirror to find out. I pulled back the covers, swung my legs over the side of the bed, and noticed they were, in fact, as thin as bones. I touched my face and went to the mirror. What I saw verified my worst fears. It had not been a dream. What I saw was horrid, so I got back in bed and started to cry.

Then, a lot of people came in and stood around me acting as if they were seeing a corpse. They no longer had masks on and I could see looks of shock on their faces. They had expected me to die. Then the most amazing thing happened; I found I could sense the thoughts and emotions of the people around me, which had never happened before. Something had happened to me when I traveled to the White Light. I had experienced a miracle and now, as a result, I was more present, more aware, and able to sense things about people I couldn't, before.

I didn't know or understand what had happened to me, but I knew it was supernatural. I had experienced a miracle. I had come back from the Light different. I was alive and had a purpose. I couldn't wait until I could talk to somebody about it because I didn't understand it. I had been to the White Light and I had been shown so many wondrous things. It didn't take long, however, to learn that if I told people something like, "I know what you're feeling" or "I know what's going to happen" or "I went to the Light," they would all just tell me, "You had a very high fever and that causes hallucinations." But I knew that

I had been touched by the Holy Spirit—and that experience has made me who I am today.

They tried to reassure me that my hair would grow back, and I would gain weight. They said my grandparents, Ma, and Pappy were going to bring me hot fudge sundaes and banana splits every night to put weight back on me. They told me my family and friends could come visit now and did what they could to make me feel better about my situation. But I was skin and bones, and I couldn't walk anymore! I knew I would have to relearn.

So, I asked for strength from whatever power had taken me to the Light, and I pulled myself up. There was a full-length window in the room and I just had to see something alive and growing, something in the light of day. But my legs were so wobbly I had to grab the back of a chair and use it as a walker to get to the window. When I got to the window, my arms went up in the air by themselves and I started praying, "Heavenly Father, what do you want from me? Why did you bring me back? What do you want me to do? Why didn't you take me?"

While my arms were up, powerful vibrations enveloped me. I felt intense sensations of gentleness, healing, and love delivered to me like a gift all tied up with a big bow. Even though it was a sunny day, an incredibly beautiful rainbow came across the sky and I tingled from head to toe. It was a tingle that gave me ultimate pleasure and reassurance. Rapid-fire images showing me all the aspects of the sanctuaries I was to create and the lives I was to touch flooded my mind at an incredible pace. I saw discord between men and women, confusion, sickness, pain—while waves of love, compassion, and trust rippled through my body and permeated my soul.

I took that rainbow, and the tingling sensation it brought me, to be a confirmation of the messages and life purpose I had received in the tunnel. It was the completion of my trans- formation. Ever since then, whenever I meet someone that I know I'm supposed to meet, I tingle like that. From that moment on I started getting stronger. I began to heal so quickly the doctors and nurses agreed it was nothing short of a miracle.

If you were to ask me what the most significant turning point in my life has been, I would have to say it was then, when I went to the White Light and my life purpose was downloaded into me. I went in as a girl and I came out a woman with a mission. That's why I'm here today. That's why I'm on this planet doing what I'm doing, creating Sanctuary wherever I can.

Our anxiety does not come from thinking about the future,
but from wanting to control it.

~ Kahlil Gibran

Chapter 2

The Problem is Stress

The earliest known sanctuary lies in the Cave of Chauvet in southern France where, around 35,000 years ago, the Aurignacian people painted images of the animals that sustained their lives. These breathtaking images are not there to decorate a living space. There is no evidence of human occupation in the cave. The Aurignacian people must have come to Chauvet for some other purpose.

All we know for sure that they did in the cave was paint—with astonishing style, sophistication, and precision—images of the animals that assured their survival. So, it seems reasonable to assume that somehow, through incantations, psychedelic sacraments or ritual frenzies, people must have used this space to supplicate, celebrate, and commune with the forces of nature. Here we can imagine them entering the Spirit world, experiencing epiphany, and undergoing transformation.

We can easily envision the Cave of Chauvet, along with similar sites such as Lascaux and Altamira, as places where Paleolithic people left the ordinary world behind. Absolute darkness and unnatural silence engulfed their senses. Sensations were heightened, perceptions stretched, anxieties suspended, stresses transcended. Flickering firelight brought the animal drawings to life. Dramatic reverberations gave songs and incantations a magical quality. The very spirit of the place was transformational.

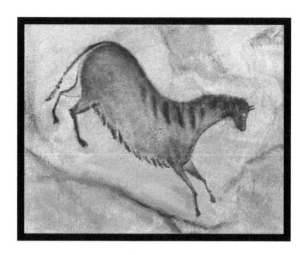

In today's world, such sanctuaries are needed more than ever before.

Life is Full of Stress

A national survey in 2017, by the American Psychological Association[1], found that:

Most Common Source of Stress:

> Eighty-three percent of us agree that stress can have deleterious effects on our health.

> Ninety-four percent—more than nine out of ten— believe stress can contribute to the development of major illnesses, such as heart disease, obesity, and depression.

Seventy-five percent of us report money as a source of stress.

Seventy percent cite work as a source of stress.

Also cited as sources of stress were the economy, relationships, health challenges, housing costs, and personal safety.

The physical symptoms of stress reported are just as wide-ranging.

Forty-two percent say they have experienced irritability or anger as a symptom of stress.

Thirty-nine percent feel nervous or anxious.

Thirty-seven percent experience fatigue.

Thirty-two percent get headaches.

Twenty-four percent experience indigestion.

Changes in appetite and sex drive are also reported as symptoms of stress.

Emotionally, stress is just as debilitating.

Thirty percent report feeling as though they could cry.

Thirty-five percent lose their energy and motivation.

Thirty-seven percent become depressed.

Forty-four percent lie awake at night.

Forty-four percent of us report that our stress is increasing.

Because of the 2020 COVID pandemic, the levels of stress and anxiety has skyrocketed while mental, physical, and emotional health have dramatically increased.

It's Only Natural

But isn't stress a natural part of life? Yes, it is. Today there are no more "natural" (or inevitable) parts of life than work and money, and the APA survey found that work and money are reported by about seventy-five percent of us to be causes of stress. More than half of us identify housing costs, workload, children, families, health concerns, and intimate relationships as causes of stress. About half of us find stress has a negative effect on personal relationships and job satisfaction. Half of all employees report having made career changes as the result of workplace stress. One in four has experienced personal alienation, separation, or divorce as a result of stress.

Stress also increases the likelihood that we will engage in unhealthy behaviors. Two-thirds of smokers report smoking more when stressed. Seventeen percent of drinkers report the same thing. And half say they lie awake at night when stressed.

So, stress can be very harmful, especially if nothing is done to relieve it. According to cellular biologist Dr. Bruce Lipton[2], the damage is done on the cellular level. In his book, *The Biology of Belief*, he tells us that our cells have two basic modes of operation: growth and protection—but they can only operate in one mode at a time. In the growth mode, the cell exchanges material with its environment freely; nutrients come in, waste products go out, the cell performs its function as it should, and reproduces itself before it wears out.

When the protection mode activates in response to a perceived threat, internal or external, growth processes screech to a halt. This is the mode that stress puts us in—and it's a completely natural reaction. When facing a hungry lion, you need every speck of your energy, attention, and physical anticipation focused exclusively on the lion. In response to hormones produced by the pituitary and adrenal glands, cells retreat within themselves, stop exchanging with their environments, build up toxic wastes, and stop dividing. If it goes on long enough, the cell dies.

If we don't manage the stress in our lives, it can literally destroy us. We know that. But we also know that stress is a natural and inescapable part of life. So, what's a person to do?

The Way Out of Stress

If you go to your family physician with stress related symptoms, it is likely your physician will prescribe a tranquilizer, an antidepressant, or some other pharmaceutical. Drug therapy has been effective for many people, especially those suffering the most severe symptoms. But pharmaceuticals all have side effects, both short and long-term. Some of them interact badly with other drugs. Some can be addictive, and some can cause lasting damage.

17

Strenuous exercise has also been shown to be effective in reducing stress and everyone should be encouraged to include a good exercise regimen in their daily schedule. But, as everyone who's ever tried it knows, daily exercise programs take a lot of discipline, special clothes and equipment, maybe membership in a gym—and a more reliably routine life than most of us can manage. If you like to walk or run, weather can be a factor. No wonder most of us simply find it impractical to implement such a discipline on the daily basis required for optimal results.

Yoga, meditation, tai chi, and other mind/body practices have also been shown to be effective in diminishing the effects of stress. But these practices also require a degree of discipline that many of us find daunting. Learning any of these practices requires instruction from a qualified teacher and takes an extended period of time. These practices are also, in their own ways, quite strenuous.

Listening to music and reading are the most often cited ways people say they try to reduce stress. But listening to music in the car or reading on the train won't reduce much stress. Of course, it also matters what you listen to or read. Each of us is different but certain musical frequencies have been shown to cause brain waves to be generated of a frequency that is beneficial in reducing stress. And it is difficult to imagine that reading a book about war, for example, would reduce more stress than a book about the joy of being alive. To be effective at reducing stress, these practices must be done in a quiet, peaceful place that cultivates relaxation and healing.

That's what a Sanctuary is.

Within you there is a stillness
and a sanctuary to which you can
retreat at any time and be yourself.

~ Hermann Hesse

Chapter 3

The Solution is Sanctuary

The dictionary defines sanctuary as "a sacred place; a place set apart as a refuge; a safe haven." As we shall use the term, Sanctuary is that and much more. Sanctuary is a place conducive to mental, physical, and emotional renewal; a comfortably furnished space with soft light, soothing music, pleasing scents, and a peaceful ambiance. It is a place designed for relaxing and refreshing both mind and body. And we shall also expand the term "sanctuary" not only to describe a place, but the state of mind that place induces: a state of tranquil serenity, natural bliss, and spiritual expansion.

The size of a sanctuary space is not important but how that space is appointed is of critical importance. An effective sanctuary features a number of elements, each of which contributes to the overall effect of the space in a different way.

Furniture – A Sanctuary space needs to have a place to sit, recline or lie down comfortably—but not so comfortably that it encourages sleep. Sanctuary furniture should allow someone to remain comfortably quiet and still for a significant period of time. This can be a chair, a sofa or just a sitting cushion, depending on the needs and tastes of the user. Notice that I said "a" chair, sofa, or cushion, as in "one." We'll look at why that's important a little later.

Lighting – Human beings are highly sensitive to light. The coming and going of daylight paces our lives. We have evolved to react to that. Recent studies[3] have indicated that incandescent light at low illumination levels enhances relaxation and daylight improves attention levels. Bright light treats jet lag by resetting our internal clock to a new morning. Low-level lighting simulates the coming of evening, signaling our bodies that it's time to wind down. The warm color of firelight enhances this effect.

Candles – Anyone who has ever spent time next to a campfire knows the mind stilling effect of an open flame. As the captivated camper watches the fire burn and dance, the rest of the world and all its cares, literally and figuratively, disappear. Candlelight offers a similar potential. The flickering of a single flame focuses the mind away from all the sources of stress that plague our consciousness on a daily basis. That's a great start to purging stress completely. For extra safety, I'd recommend using candles in glass containers.

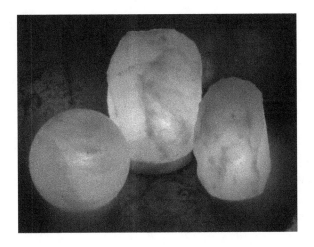

Salt Lamps – Himalayan salt lamps are hollowed out chunks of rock salt, either carved or left natural, with low wattage light bulbs inside. The warm, soft light that filters through the salt is both beautiful and beneficial. As the light bulbs heat the salt, it gives off negative chlorine ions that bond with dust, pollen, dander, and other irritants in the air, weighing the particles down until gravity pulls them down. Approved for use in the treatment of allergies by the USDA, salt lamps clean the air, ease allergy symptoms, and make relaxing that much easier.

Music – The effects of music on mental, emotional, and physical well-being are perhaps more dramatic than any other element of sanctuary. Allowing patients to listen to music of their choice during medical procedures has been shown to reduce pain[4], decrease anxiety levels[5], and lower sedation requirements[6]. For women who underwent mastectomies, when music was played[7] throughout the preoperative, intra-operative, and postoperative periods experienced a greater decrease in MAP *(mean arterial pressure)*, anxiety, and pain, than a control group of those for whom no music was played.

EEG studies have shown that music can decrease the bioelectrical activity in the brain from predominantly beta waves to alpha and theta waves, which have important consequences for the reduction of anxiety, tension, and sleeplessness[8].

And the list goes on. The National Center for Biotechnology Information's website lists more than 14,000 peer reviewed studies investigating the effects of music on the human mind and body. To induce the "sanctuary effect" of stress reduction, recovery, and renewal there are three basic types of music to consider:

> ***Soothing*** – The most important factor in selecting music that soothes and relaxes the listener is rhythm. The most calming pace lies in the range of fifty to seventy beats a minute, the rate of a healthy human heart. Sixty to eighty beats per minute is considered "uplifting" in its effects, and also appropriate for sanctuary. Music with faster rhythms induces too much energy for relaxation. Music with a rhythm below fifty beats a minute induces sleep.
>
> Simplicity is important as well. Music is most relaxing when there are no lyrics to follow. And instrumentation should be limited. Complex orchestral music requires energetic listening. Soothing music includes music from the meditation, easy listening, soft jazz, and chamber music genres, along with a great array of music that defies categorization.
>
> ***Inspirational*** – For many people, spending time in Sanctuary is a spiritual experience. For these people, spiritual music may be the most effective genre for

relieving stress. In this circumstance, simple devotional lyrics may be beneficial, but instrumentation should still be limited, and rhythms kept in the "soothing" range.

Entraining – Some music is designed to use the "frequency following" tendency of the human brain to generate brainwaves that mimic frequencies in the music. In a process known as "brainwave entrainment," these frequencies cause the brain to generate alpha, theta and/or delta brainwaves. When our brains are generating alpha waves, we feel calm and alert. We think more clearly and make better decisions with better long-term results. We have emotional flexibility and a better command of our lives, health, and moods.

When we generate theta brainwaves, we enter the deepest state of relaxation, mentally free and highly creative. It's the state we enter as we fall asleep or gradually awaken. Frequencies that generate delta waves induce sleep.

To generate these beneficial stress beating brainwaves, binaural beats, monaural beats, and isochronic tones of the proper frequencies are built into the music. Binaural beats are created when two tones close in frequency are played together and the brain "hears" a subaudible beat equal to the frequency difference between the two. Monaural beats, which can be heard, are created when two tones of similar amplitude are played together, producing a beat when the frequencies overlap. Isochronic beats are produced when a frequency is turned on and off in rapid succession. When these beats are timed properly, the brain generates alpha and theta waves that sync up with the beats.

Music that incorporates binaural, monaural, and iso-chronic beats is sold as brainwave entrainment, meditation, or relaxation music.

Sound Therapy – uses various instruments like drums, rattles, crystal bowls, Tibetan Singing Bowls, tuning forks, and chimes. The frequencies have a powerful effect on you, as it breaks up the negative emotions and energy in your body which can assist your body to come back into balance.

You may also use lighter sounds to calm, relax, and release stress such as listening to the sound of ocean waves, and the trickle of raindrops.

Sound therapy has been used for centuries by various cultural groups, but it's just become popular in Western culture in the last few decades.

Silence – Music is not the only auditory stimulation that has been shown to reduce stress. Simple, ordinary silence, the stimulation you get when all other sounds have ceased, also has the power to lower blood pressure, slow breathing, and reduce anxiety.

A 2015 study* conducted at the Penn State College of Medicine found that postoperative subjects who wore noise cancelling headphones for thirty minutes just after surgery experienced reduced heart rates and lower pain scores as compared to baseline measurements. As a result, the study concluded that "noise reduction could decease opioid administration, promote relaxation, and improve patient satisfaction."

A 2006 study** found that silence lowers blood cortisol and adrenaline, which can lower blood pressure and improve blood circulation to the brain. The study reported just two minutes of silence to be more relaxing than listening to music. A 2013 study*** published in *Brain Structure and Function* found that two hours of silence increased the production of brain cells.

Silence has also been credited with boosting the body's immune system, improving hormone regulation, and decreasing arterial plaque formation. Almost any activity conducted in silence becomes more focused and more effective. It is especially effective at enhancing meditation, prayer, or yoga.

The noise pollution we are all immersed in every day has been shown to induce stress reactions linked to heart disease, high blood pressure, stroke, and compromised immune responses. So, spending some time each day in silence as part of your Sanctuary practice is highly recommended. As an alternative to music for its own rewards, in a Sanctuary setting, silence truly is golden.

Aroma – Herbal aromas have been used for centuries to soothe and heal a wide variety of ailments and conditions. These aromas are produced by diffusing essential oils extracted from a variety of plants into the air, either through burning or evaporation. These oils consist of molecules small enough to pass across the blood-brain barrier, giving our brains more protection than the rest of the body from blood-borne bacteria, viruses, and toxins; so they produce beneficial effects quickly.

The list of herbs and plants used in aromatherapy is vast. Peppermint is used to treat headaches and digestive distress. Eucalyptus is used for coughs, colds, and other respiratory problems. Geranium helps balance female hormones and is sometimes used as an antidepressant. Tea tree oil is a natural antifungal agent; lemon and rosemary are uplifting; clary sage is a natural painkiller.

But possibly the most frequent use of therapeutic aromas lies in the reduction of stress and treatment of the symptoms of stress. Sandalwood, marjoram, ylang ylang and lavender are commonly used to reduce anxiety, muscle tension, and mental hyperactivity. Chamomile is relaxing to the point of being used as a sleep aid.

Scientific evidence of the effectiveness of aromatherapy is abundant. Studies have shown aromatherapy to reduce stress levels in subjects as diverse as teenagers[9] and dementia patients[10]. In addition to reducing pain and muscular spasms, calming, and assisting sleep, lavender has been shown to reduce inflammation[11]. Sweet orange has shown great promise in the treatment of anxiety disorders[12]. And a pilot study has shown aromatherapy to be effective even in the treatment of such difficult conditions as postpartum depression[13]. Therapeutic aromas are an essential element of Sanctuary.

Incense and Scented Candles – Incense is a time-honored method of putting beneficial aromas into the air. It has been used to create peaceful frames of mind since the Stone Age. The pungent fragrance of incense is so effective at inducing calmness of mind that, after a time, just the scent of it becomes a trigger for relaxation responses. Scented candles do much the same thing, although some people are sensitive to both incense and candle aromas. Soy candles are the healthier choice as they burn cleaner than other wax candles.

Essential Oils – Essential oils are commonly used by sprinkling the oils onto the palms, rubbing the palms together, placing the palms close to the nose, and inhaling deeply. But essential oils can be suffused into the entire atmosphere of a Sanctuary by evaporative diffusers that electrically heat the oils to accelerate their evaporation. Diffusers that use wicks to absorb and evaporate essential oils can also be effective, without using electricity.

Essential oils include:

Allspice Berry	Citronella	Lavender	Peru Balsam
Amyris	Clary Sage	Lemon	Pine
Anise	Clove Bud	Eucalyptus	Rose
Basil	Coriander Seed	Lemongrass	Rosemary
Bay	Cypress	Lime	Rosewood
Bergamot	Eucalyptus	Mandarin	Sandalwood
Camphor	Fennel	Marjoram	Spearmint
Cardamom Seed	Frankincense	Moringa	Spruce
Carrot Seed	Geranium	Myrrh	Sweet Tangerine
Cassia Bark	Ginger	Myrtle	Tea Tree
Cedar	Grapefruit	Neroli	Thyme
Chamomile	Hyssop	Nutmeg	Vanilla
Cinnamon Bark	Jasmine	Orange	Vetiver
Cinnamon Leaf	Juniper Berry	Oregano	Wintergreen
	Lavandin	Palmarosa	Ylang Ylang
		Patchouli	
		Peppermint	

Below is a brief description of some of the more common essential oils used:

Basil – improves concentration, alertness, memory retention, digestive system, respiratory, sinus congestion, and nausea.

Chamomile Roman – peaceful, calming, reduces stress and anxiety, and promotes restful sleep. Anti-inflammatory, and often used as a balm for muscle soreness, spasms, and joint pain. Soothing on insect bites.

Eucalyptus radiate – beneficial for the respiratory system, clearing sinuses, reliving sinus pressure, and reducing headaches. Also, can help with mental exhaustion, muscle aches, and abdominal or menstrual cramping.

Ginger – relieves jet lag, motion sickness, and nausea.

Grapefruit – aids in mental exhaustion, jet lag, skin care as a natural astringent and can help improve skin tone, elasticity, blemish prone, and congested or oily skin. Good for muscle fatigue and stiffness, as well as immune support.

Lavender – use for first aid—minor wounds like bruises, burns, cuts and scrapes, bug bites, and sunburn. Also, used for relaxation, easing headaches, promotes restful steep. Skin care—anti-inflammatory and regenerative properties help sooth irritated and sensitive skin.

Moringa – contains sterols, which have been shown to lower LDL or "bad" cholesterol. Moringa oil contains several bioactive compounds, which have antioxidant and anti-inflammatory properties, both when ingested and used topically. Beneficial for acne breakouts.

Orange – helps alleviate tension and stress, fight fatigue, boost mental clarity, and encourage a positive outlook. Promotes better digestion, relives indigestion, and cramping. Helps rid the body of toxins and fluid accumulation.

Peppermint – increase focus, mental clarity, memory, alertness, and concentration while soothing nervous stress. One of the best essential oils to relieve headaches, nasal and respiratory congestion, digestive problems like bloating, cramping, nausea, motion sickness, and upset stomach. It nourishes dry skin and can be used in hair care to relieve scalp irritation and dryness, stimulate hair growth, and give hair a shiny, fresh look. Peppermint is also known to deter mice, ants, and spiders. AVOID EYE CONTACT AND MAKE SURE YOU WASH YOUR HANDS AFTER USING PEPPERMINT OIL.

Rose – relive stress and nervous tension, boost confidence, self-esteem, and mental strength. Excellent for skin care. Rose works to balance hormones and support female reproductive health by relieving cramping, nausea, pain, and fatigue related to menstruation.

Rosemary – stimulating effect on the brain, improves cognitive function by increasing concentration, focus clarity, and memory retention.

Tea Tree – a must have essential oil for every home first aid kit. Prevents infection and speeds healing of minor cuts, scrapes, burns, bug bits, rashes, and other wounds. For skin care it helps clear pores, regulate oil production, and improve the appearance of blemishes, scars, and age spots. It is reputed to be effective against nail bed fungus, dandruff, warts, and athlete's foot. Can boost the immune system and also relieve respiratory conditions by clearing congestion and reducing inflammation and pain in the airways. Great household cleaner and shown to control mold.

Thyme – strengthens a healthy immune system and prevents infections. Boosts circulation, aids toxin removal, and acts as an anti-inflammatory to help sooth minor aches and pains.

Color – The color of a sanctuary is just as important as the scent. The fact that color affects human well-being has been known for centuries[14]. In ancient Egypt and Greece color—in the form of colored garments, oils, plasters, ointments and salves—was used to treat disease by restoring natural balance. While they do not address the issue of natural balance, modern scientific studies have verified that colors do, indeed, have significant effects on human well-being.

It turns out that our physical reactions to various colors are closely related to how we feel about those colors—and how we feel about a color seems to be cued by what we associate that color with. In other words, we tend to like colors associated with things we like and dislike colors associated with things we dislike[15]. These associations tend to be hardwired into our psyches by generations of experience.

For example, exposure to the color blue, the color of a clear sky, or a body of life-giving water, has been shown to reduce blood pressure and slow respiration[16].

The color green, the color of the earth in its season of plenty, evokes positive emotions, relaxation, and comfort. Green-yellow, on the other hand, tends to be associated with feelings of sickness and disgust[17]. There is considerable individual variation in color associations and preferences but, in general; blue, blue-green, green, red-purple, purple, and purple-blue tend to be seen as the most pleasant colors[18].

Color also has effects on human perception and behavior. In one study, taste was perceived as being nearly one-and-a-half times sweeter in red light than in white or green light[19]. Jailhouse pink, also known as "tranquilizing pink", is a shade of pink that reduces aggressiveness by suppressing the secretion of aggression hormones. It has been successfully used to lower inmate aggression in criminal holding facilities all across the country.

Blue, the shortest wavelength in the spectrum of visible light, tens to receded from the eye, so blue surfaces tend to be perceived as further away than they really are, whereas longer wavelength red surfaces tend to be perceived as closer. That means rooms painted in a color that is toward the blue end of the visible light spectrum (violets, blues, and greens) tend to be perceived as more spacious than rooms painted in a color that is toward the red end of the spectrum.

There are many different descriptions of the qualities and associations attached to various colors and most of them overlap to one degree or another. The list below contains some of the most common denominators:

Aquamarine – The color aquamarine is a combination of yellow, blue, and green that is associated with healing. It is said to encourage emotions that support balance and stability but,

34

in an aquamarine environment, a person may experience a cascade of emotions before equanimity is realized.

Black – is a glamorous color that absorbs and consolidates all the others. It stands for timeless style. It is a serious color that represents breaking free from bad habits and addictions. Although associated with mourning and depression, black evokes emotions that can help people feel pure and open. It is said to open up deep unconscious thought processes.

Blue – has a soothing effect on human nerves, inducing peace and calm. It creates a comforting space with a feeling of "coolness" that brings tranquility and relieves stress. It is said to reduce inflammation, fever, high blood pressure, headaches, as well as strong emotions like anger, aggression, or hysteria. It promotes peace and rest, a sense of order, logic, and rational thinking.

Brown – is a warm color, with some shades suggesting sophistication and elegance. It is a serious color: practical, reliable, sensible, and wholesome. The color promotes a sense of emotional safety, household protection, and prosperity. It is said to increase decisiveness and attract help in financial crises.

Gold – is the color of wealth and prosperity. It is said to promote health, endurance and cheerfulness, abundance, wisdom, and deep understanding. Gold promotes energy and inspiration and is said to be helpful in counteracting fear and hesitation.

Green – is associated with nature and has a calming effect on the mind and body. It nurtures refreshment, restoration, and equilibrium. Used to treat stress and anxiety, the color creates a relaxed atmosphere, and promotes a sense of prosperity and abundance. Said to bring psychological and emotional harmony, green is the color of balance, peace, rest, hope, and comfort.

Indigo – is said to instill feelings of stillness, internal peace, serenity, and heightened creativity. It is associated with intuition and higher levels of perception and consciousness. It is also linked to sincerity, integrity, wisdom, and fairness.

Magenta – is associated with feelings of internal relaxation, universal harmony, and emotional balance. Both spiritual and practical, it encourages common sense and a balanced outlook on life. This is a color that helps to create balance and harmony in every aspect of life; physically, mentally, emotionally, and spiritually.

Orange – is a warm, cheery, non-constricting color that has a freeing effect upon the body and mind. It stimulates creative thinking and enthusiasm, helps assimilate new ideas and moderates excessive sexual expression. Representing the warmth of the fire, orange is said to promote energy, comfort, celebration, abundance, and enjoyment of the senses.

Pink – symbolizes softness, sweetness, innocence, youthful-ness, and tenderness. It calms agitation and gives rise to feelings of hope, physical tranquility, warmth, and love. Pink is said to heal grief and sadness, restore youthfulness, and put you in contact with your feelings. Pink is used to create an atmos-phere of sophistication, health, and strength.

Purple – is a color of transformation, half red and half blue, and represents the unity of dualities. It is said to induce sleep and soothe mental and emotional stress. This color promotes contemplation and spiritual reflection. It is the color of dignity and extrasensory perception.

Red – is associated with love, passion, ferocity, and boldness. This color promotes energy, strength, willpower, and brilliance, raises energy levels, creates excitement, and stimulates conversation. It is used to treat low energy, fatigue, and colds, warm the chilly and embolden the passive. It is said to energize heart and blood circulation, stimulate the organs, and energize the senses and increase sexual desire.

Silver – is a color of prestige, dignity, and practicality. It promotes modesty, persistence, and reliability, evokes a sense of peace and calm, and adds a sleek, cool atmosphere.

Teal – is a color of relaxation and unwinding. It can help to regain balance and harmony after a stressful and challenging day. Teal is a medium to deep blue-green color made by combining blue and green pigments in a white base. This calm and peaceful color represents feelings of restorative rejuvenation. As in all colors, different shades will resonate with different people. Use the particular shades that resonates with you.

Turquoise – is a combination of blue and a small amount of yellow that is said to facilitate open communication and clarity of thought while strengthening the connection between the heart and the spoken word. It is a friendly and happy color that radiates peace, calm, and tranquility. Turquoise is also known to stimulate and enhance emotions that create balance and inner harmony.

White – is associated with simplicity, purity, and cleanliness, perfect balance and harmony. It promotes feelings of protection, encouragement, order, and efficiency. Considered to be the color of the Awakened Spirit and Divine Light, white is said to raise consciousness and bring harmony to all aspects of life.

Yellow – is the color of the sun, vitality, and energy. It stimulates optimism, well-being, self-esteem, and emotional strength. The color is said to strengthen the nerves and the mind, awaken mental inspiration, and stimulate higher mentality, promoting cheerfulness, curiosity, flexibility, and learning. Although yellow can give rise to negative emotions like fear and anxiety, it can also lift our spirits, generate new ideas and clarify thoughts.

> *Wall Color* – Sanctuaries are places of peace, relaxation, and well-being. The colors that evoke those feelings best are the colors of the shorter wavelengths, the colors that remind us of blue skies and green meadows. In general, lighter shades are more relaxing than more saturated shades, sky blue is more relaxing than royal blue, seafoam green more relaxing than Kelly green. Short wavelength colors also recede from the eye, tend to be perceived as further away and make a room seem more spaciousness.

> *Fabrics, Furnishings and Floor* – The fabrics, furnishings, and floor covering of a sanctuary should also be selected to enhance feelings of peace, relaxation, and well-being. The floor covering should be of a color that complements the wall color and of a texture comfortable to bare feet. The color may be blended but prints or patterns should be avoided. Curtains and accent swags should be of light, free-flowing fabrics that evoke lightness of being. Natural fibers should be used in preference to synthetic fabrics whenever possible. Furniture, which should be kept sparse, should feature simple, elegant lines, comfortable padding, soft texture, and a solid color harmonious with the walls and floor covering. And all the furnishings should be arranged to foster the greatest possible perception of elegant simplicity.

Nature – There's nothing like a day in the country to ease the mind and lift the spirits. The therapeutic benefits of natural scenes and settings seem built into the human psyche. In a study that exposed subjects suffering from stress to the sight of either natural or urban environments, the subjects exposed to the natural environments recovered faster[20]. Another study showed that exposure to natural scenes caused subjects to generate more alpha waves than when shown urban scenes[21]. Surgery patients exposed to nature scenes experienced less pain and recovered more quickly.

For Sanctuaries, the most important information to be gained from scientific studies is the fact that exposure to nature and representations of nature reduce stress[23]. A beautiful landscape outside a clean window is ideal—but the soothing effects of nature can also be evoked through room accents, sights, and sounds that trigger this "natural" stress reduction. Like furnishings, accent elements should be selected and placed with an eye toward simplicity and elegance.

In Sanctuary, less is more.

> *Flowers* – Fresh flowers trigger springtime emotional reactions, represented by feelings of hope and optimism. From a spray of color in a window box to a single bloom in a simple vase, fresh flowers bring the renewing energy of springtime to all who enter.

> *Plants* – The presence of living plants has also been shown to reduce stress[24]. For Sanctuaries, the number and type of plants should be determined by the light available and placed with a priority on simple elegance. Once properly selected and carefully placed, a single plant is more effective than plants all around the room.

Birdsong – Birdsong heralds spring and triggers springtime responses. Plants grow more vigorously when birdsongs are played. Humans relax and smile. Kept at a volume just loud enough to be heard in the background, whether from a CD or an environmental sound device, birdsong is a small accent that makes a big difference.

Aquariums – Aquariums require maintenance – but who among us has never been fascinated by one? The Neurobehavioral Research Laboratory and Clinic reports that as little as five minutes contact with an aquarium can "significantly decrease stress, reduce anger and fear, and increase pleasant feelings." The logistics of maintenance notwithstanding, aquariums are powerful stress reducers.

Flowing Water – The sound of flowing water is one of the most soothing sounds there is, a sound that washes away the noise of our chattering minds and overstuffed lives. It's a sound that takes us away from the chaos and strife of everyday living and transports us to a more peaceful place. The most effective source of flowing water sounds is a strategically placed, electrically powered waterfall—but recorded sounds can also be effective.

Art – Like all Sanctuary accents, artwork should be selected and placed according to the "less is more" principle. One or two paintings or photographs of natural landscapes is enough. Human figures in the artwork are not recommended. It's the perception and associations of nature that bring us stress relief.

Solitude – Sanctuary is a solitary experience. There's a lot to be said for the company of others but solitude offers unique benefits for anyone seeking to reduce stress. *Psychology Today* reports that spending time alone allows us to unwind our minds. Without distractions, you can clear your mind, focus your thoughts, and think more clearly. Like muddy water clears when left alone, the residual effects of allowing your thoughts to settle are improved concentration and increased productivity. Solitude allows you to discover your own thoughts, free from the distractions and influences of the thoughts of others. Studies have shown that when we are alone, we think more deeply, are more creative, make better choices, and solve problems more effectively. Although some people may see wanting to spend time alone as the mark of someone who is sad, lonely, or antisocial, it is actually a healthy and highly beneficial thing to do in your own sanctuary.

Journaling – Journaling is a great way to become aware of your stress. There is something about writing worrisome thoughts and feelings down on paper that clarifies and objectifies them so that we can see them, acknowledge them, and put them in perspective. It's a way to process negative or traumatic emotions, and let a more positive perspective emerge[25], a way to reflect and analyze and find patterns in your life, and resolve long-standing challenges.

Journaling regularly has been shown to strengthen the immune system, ease the symptoms of asthma, arthritis, and other conditions, improve cognitive function, and counteract the effects of stress[26]. But, even on an occasional basis, journaling provides a way to express anger or frustration that is safe and nonconfrontational. Writing involves both hemispheres of the brain, so journaling fully integrates what we write into our thought process.

Sanctuary is the perfect place for journaling; quiet, peaceful, and mentally relaxing. To accommodate journaling, a Sanctuary should have a writing surface, either a laptop or a small, simple desk, and a place to discreetly store writing materials. Although computers are generally discouraged at Sanctuary, journaling may be the one purpose for which they may be beneficial. Some of us just couldn't do it any other way.

Inspiration – For many, Sanctuary is a place for spiritual renewal; a place to pray, meditate, or just contemplate the wonders of life. For these people, it is appropriate that a few select inspirational touchstones, such as books and/or icons, be included in Sanctuary.

Books – For most Americans, the inspirational book of choice is the Bible. For others, it might be the Torah, the Qur'an, the Vedas, or the Sutras. For those of more contemporary spirituality, it might be the works of philosophers, shamans, or sages. The choices are unlimited—and entirely individual.

Icons – Icons symbolize entire belief systems, like books expressed as sculpture. They can trigger long cascades of thought and inspiration, creating an atmosphere of reverence, a sense of higher purpose, and an expectation that, in Sanctuary, stress will be transcended.

Remember,
the entrance door
to the sanctuary
is inside you.

~ Rumi

Chapter 4

A Sanctuary of Your Own

Turning Space into Sanctuary — In a world that is busy always doing, each of us needs a personal space where we can put our to-do list on hold and nurture our well-being. Whether you're in abundant health or challenged with a health conflict, surrounding yourself with beauty, relaxing music, and nature is a precious gift, perhaps the most generous gift you can give yourself. It is the currency for peace of mind, love, compassion, and forgiveness. Living with these qualities allows you to live in higher awareness.

The quality of life we create for ourselves makes us who we are. Peaceful surroundings promote peace of mind. Imagine yourself living in a relaxed, rejuvenated, and truly peaceful frame of mind. In your Sanctuary your mind can be clear, your body relaxed, and your spiritual essence renewed. In this space, you are empowered to be the best possible you.

Once you have created your sacred space, you can enjoy a blissful sense of surrender and begin to truly appreciate your life. There is so much to be grateful for, no matter what your situation happens to be. Sanctuary allows you the time and space to experience that gratitude. It is a safe place to feel present in your own life; a place where you can feel the heart-beat of the Universe beating in your own chest; a place of peace, tranquility, and comfort at all levels—heaven on earth.

Ten Steps to Creating Your Own Sanctuary

Step One: Claim Your Space – Sanctuary does not have to occupy a large amount of space. A spare bedroom is wonderful but a utility room, storage space, converted garage, a partitioned off portion in a larger room, or even an outdoor space can be just as effective. It is important, however, that you create your Sanctuary in a place that's quiet, or can be made quiet, and has a comfortable airflow.

Now claim your Sanctuary space by making a commitment to use it exclusively for the enhancement of your well-being. It is important that each time you go into your Sanctuary, you enter with a Sanctuary mindset that lets go of stress and embraces tranquility. Each time you enter your Sanctuary with this mindset, it reinforces your expectations of well-being and enhances your Sanctuary's effectiveness. Using your Sanctuary space for any other purpose dilutes this effect and works at cross-purposes to the process of Sanctuary.

Once you've claimed your space, take a "before" picture of it. The benefits of this step come under the heading of self-reward. It's a two-step process whose payoff doesn't kick in until step nine, but don't neglect this step. It's impact on you and your mindset can be delightful!

Step Two: Sage Smudging – Once you've claimed your Sanctuary space, it is highly recommended that you smudge it with a smoldering bundle of white sage or white prairie sage. The smoke of burning sage has been used for centuries by Native Americans and other traditional cultures to cleanse ceremonial spaces of negative energies, repel insects, can reduce mood disorders, anxiety, and depression. Science has validated the therapeutic value of sage in 2016 when a research project at the University of Mississippi[27] found that white sage contains compounds that activate receptors in the brain responsible for regulating moods, reducing stress, and relieving pain.

The smoke of white sage contains chemical compounds that possess strong antioxidant, and antibacterial properties. It also contains compounds that are thought to enhance cognitive activity and protect against neurodegenerative disease. A review of the scientific literature published in *Drugs RD*[28] cites multiple studies that indicated sage may offer benefits for memory, attention, and learning. It is even thought to hold promise for the treatment of dementia and Alzheimer's disease.

So, for a variety of reasons, smudging your space with smoldering white or white prairie sage is a highly valuable enhancement to your Sanctuary space. Use it before you do anything else, then use it each time you use your Sanctuary.

For your safety and protection, please be extra cautious with the smudging process, so that no embers get on your rugs, clothing, etc.

Step Three: Clear Your Slate – The first physical task in turning a space into a sanctuary is to clear the space out completely. While you're at it, take a close look at everything you're clearing out. Is it stuff you really need? Have you touched it in the last two years? The last five? Or is it just clutter? If it's clutter, put it in a special pile, and we'll talk more about that later. The important thing for now is to empty out your sanctuary space so that you can start with a clean slate, both physically and mentally.

Step Four: Set Your Intentions - Once your space is empty, go in, still yourself, and set your intentions for the space. Envision what your Sanctuary will look like when it's finished. Take your time. Envision what you will do for your Sanctuary experience, how you will do it, the space and furnishings it will require. Give some thought to colors, fabrics, art, and other aspects of the visual environment. Think about the placement of lighting and sound systems. Then draw your vision out as a floor plan and hold the image of your finished sanctuary in your mind as you go about making it happen.

Step Five: Paint Your Sanctuary – Paint your sanctuary with love. The color scheme you select is up to you. The psychological effects of various colors were discussed in the previous chapter. Choose a color and shade that you find relaxing, one that makes you feel calm and quiet, then prepare your surfaces, and apply the paint with the same care and attention to detail you would apply to a work of art. It's all about your intentions. The more care you take, the more you will appreciate your sanctuary—and yourself—every time you enter. Please note that it can also be beneficial to add your favorite essential oils to the paint, before painting.

Step Six: Select Your Furnishings – Select your Sanctuary furnishings with the awareness that less is more. Select only what you need, whether that's a bookcase and reading chair, a writing desk, or just a meditation cushion. Choose flooring and furnishings of colors that are compatible with the color of the walls. Make sure your seating is comfortable enough for extended use but not so comfortable that you fall sleep—unless napping is part of your intentions!

Indirect lighting is preferable to direct lighting except for reading light. If there are unwanted sounds coming in from outside, choose a natural sound generator that replaces those sounds with a white noise effect, such as sounds of the ocean or flowing water. And find a silent fan to keep the air moving without distraction.

Step Seven: Place Your Furnishings – Place your furnishings as though you were positioning the elements of an art exhibit. Use your floor plan as a guide, but remain flexible. If an alternative placement feels better in the finished out room, give it a try. If you've followed the principle of less is more, it won't be hard to try several configurations and find the arrangement that feels best to you.

Step Eight: Fine Tune Your Environment – Once you have everything in place, give your sanctuary a test run. Leave the space and close the door, curtain, or screen, and then enter the space from outside. How does it feel when you step in? Do you feel like exhaling? Do the muscles in your shoulders relax? Then try it out. Perform your practice: read, pray, stretch, or just sit. Does the space function the way you want it to? Do you feel differently after you've been there for a while; calmer, less stressed? If you do, you're there; if not, make adjustments—to the sounds, the music, the placement of art, or any of the other elements until tranquility ensues.

Step Nine: Take an "After" Picture – Here's where the "before" picture we recommended that you take in Step One pays off. Take an "after" picture of your finished Sanctuary and compare it to the picture you took earlier. As you delight in the transformation, know that it is symbolic of the transformation that is already taking place within you as you begin living the Sanctuary lifestyle. Take it as a measure of what you can do, on your own initiative, to enhance and maintain your well-being.

Step Ten: Issue Yourself a Passport of Permission —
The single greatest barrier to personal healing is often your own
mindset. Most of us have a guilty aversion to indulging
ourselves in personal pleasure, even if that pleasure is therapeutic. The key to healing is therefore often your own ability to
simply give yourself permission to feel good. For many, it
represents a more positive—and radically new—outlook on life.
Giving yourself a Passport of Permission acts as a tangible
symbol that you can use to bypass your own natural resistance
to change.

*A happy life consists
in tranquility of mind.*

~ Cicero

Chapter 5

Living in Sanctuary

A Sanctuary Makeover – The environment you're in affects your state of mind you're in. That's a basic principle of Sanctuary—and it can not only be applied to an exclusively dedicated space, but to every room in your home. I'm not suggesting that every room can or should be converted into Sanctuary. You still have to have a place to pay your bills, wash your clothes, and eat your dinner. But the effects of colors, aromas, and the other elements of Sanctuary can be used to make any space less stressful, more relaxing, and more nurturing. By applying the principles of Sanctuary to your whole home, you can expand Sanctuary from a space into a lifestyle.

Clutter – Start by taking a look around. If you're like most of us, what you see will not be in perfect order. Whether it's a little or a lot, there will be clutter. There will be stuff piled on a table, stacked on a credenza, overflowing a bookcase, or even strewn on the floor. Though it may have been placed there only on a temporary basis, the visual pollution clutter creates is current and ongoing. Continually seeing items in need of being put away, organized, tidied up, or cleaned can be psychologically overwhelming and lead to chronic feelings of fatigue, anxiety, and depression—like living with a great big "to-do" list in front of you wherever you look.

Taking on your clutter, especially if it's been accumulating for some time, may be something you've put off more than once. But that only makes things worse, doesn't it? Because now you have feelings of guilt to add to the mix, right? So here are some tips for making the task less frustrating:

Time It – Clear your clutter for a designated period of time each day. Whether it's fifteen minutes or an hour a day, one step at a time will take you a thousand miles. Doing a task or project in twenty-minute segments has been found to be beneficial. When you know going in that you'll only be doing this for a specific amount of time each day makes the task much more approachable.

Limit It – Deal with your stuff one room at a time. Just like a time limit, a space limit gives you goals that you can clearly see and accomplish without feeling overwhelmed.

Dance It – Have fun with your process. Put on some music while you clean and clear. You'll be amazed at how much easier and more enjoyable your work becomes. Get into the rhythm of it; make your movements into a dance and use the energy of the music to turn your work into pleasure. You may not want to stop, but don't overdo it. Creating your Sanctuary is a process that should be enjoyable.

Multi-task It — Whenever you get a couple of minutes to spare—waiting on hold, listening to an endless phone menu, talking to a friend, or whatever—clear, organize, or clean a small space, maybe just an end table or a counter top. You will be amazed at how much you can get done in the course of a day this way.

Once you've decided how you will approach clearing your clutter, you'll need to decide what to do with it as you clear it. Putting it all into the attic or a storage unit is not a good solution because, although out of sight, your stuff may not be out of mind. Just knowing that it's still there, still awaiting a final resolution, can still be a source of anxiety. What I recommend instead is taking a hard look at your stuff as you clear it and making the hard decision, piece by piece, what to do with it on a permanent basis. For that, you'll need three boxes and a lot of determination.

Put it Away – Put things you use and things you love in this box(es). Then *put it away*—in a closet, garage, attic, or storage space—clearly labeled, and easily accessible. It is also a good idea to put a date on your box label(s). That way, if you find you haven't touched a box in two years (or five years or ten years), you can rationally consider reclassifying what's inside.

Give It Away – Those things that you no longer want but are still useful, you may want to give away. This is a noble intention but it requires follow through. Don't wait for friends or relatives to come get things they may want. Take it or ship it to them immediately. The same goes for donations to charity. Get it done. Every day it sits around waiting to be delivered makes it easier for it to still be there the next day.

Throw It Away – A lot of your clutter may be stuff that, when you are honest with yourself, you have to admit nobody wants. A beeper is about as useful today as a buggy whip, even if it still works perfectly, and video cassettes will not be coming back. And you will never look at those back issues of your favorite magazine ever again. Let them go. You'll find it liberating.

Keep It Away – This is not a box; it's a commitment to maintain the visual harmony of your Sanctuary. It's a commitment to put things away rather than just putting them down, not let things accumulate, and clean as you go. A rule many people use to maintain an uncluttered environment is to not bring in anything new unless something old goes out. Do this deliberately for a time and it will become a habit; embrace the habit and it will become a lifestyle.

Color – Now take a look at the colors of your home. Referring to the colors listed in Chapter Three, what states of mind are the colors of your home inducing? Are these the states of mind that you want to induce? If not, consider repainting. It's a great way to make a fresh start and make a new commitment to Sanctuary living. Ideally, the colors of room furnishings should complement the wall colors, avoiding clashing shades and conflicting hues. Consider saturated colors for furnishings and muted colors for the walls. Avoid the interaction and busyness of too many colors: one primary color complimented by no more than two accent colors is always more soothing.

Cleanliness – A clean environment cultivates a clear mind. There is just something about a place for everything and everything in its place that is inherently satisfying. It says to the mind, "All is well and as it should be. You can relax. Be at peace." If you've painted, you've already done the hardest part of cleaning up—you moved the furniture! Keeping your environment clean is much easier —but only if you clean as you go.

Try the thirty second rule: If it takes less than twenty-four seconds to clean up after a given activity, do it now. If it takes longer than that, like washing the kitchen floor or cleaning the bathtub, do it on a schedule. Knowing that you will vacuum the carpet on Saturday will bring you peace of mind throughout the week—and peace of mind is what Sanctuary is all about. It may be challenging to get on a schedule if you haven't tried that before, but after a while it will become a habit, and then a comfortable lifestyle.

Music – As discussed earlier, music has a profound effect on your state of mind. It not only makes your work easier; it also enhances your relaxation. Try soft music with dinner instead of television. Use it to set the mood when you have guests. If you have the electronics, program your system to come on just before you get home. You'll be amazed at how much that can enhance the feelings of warmth, and belonging you feel when you enter your home.

Music is a great way to end your day. Listening to soothing music at bedtime helps you relax your mind and improves your sleep. Programming energetic music to wake you up gets you up and going with a spring in your step and gives you a positive outlook on the day. Try listening to music as you cook your meals, tend your garden, or wash the dog. No task is tedious or boring or distasteful when you're living in Sanctuary.

Smells – Smells are a powerful part of our environment, for good or ill. They come in two varieties: odors and aromas. Odors, like the smell of rotting garbage, dirty clothes, wet puppies, or sweaty humans, bring stress. Those smells are instinctively unwholesome and we feel an urge to move away from them. Trying to counteract or cover up odors doesn't work. They must be eliminated. Seal up whatever is stinking, throw it out, or wash it. In this endeavor, the disciplines of cleanliness just discussed are your greatest allies.

Aromas, on the other hand, are smells that enhance your quality of life by relaxing, invigorating, or just pleasing you, as you choose. The use of candles, incense, and aromatic oils as discussed in chapter three is basic to a Sanctuary lifestyle—but here are a few advanced tips: put a cotton ball soaked in the aromatic oil of your choice in your vacuum cleaner bag and spread the aroma as you clean your carpet! At bedtime, put a little lavender in an evaporator to help you drop off to sleep. Put a drop of peppermint oil in it when you wake up to open your eyes and energize for the day! (Never touch your eyes after handling peppermint oil.)

Only the development
of compassion
and understanding for others
can bring us the tranquility
and happiness we all seek.

~ Dalai Lama XIV

Chapter 6

Sanctuary as a Spiritual Space

For many, myself included, Sanctuary is more than a way to reduce stress and promote well-being; it is a spiritual experience. The link between physical and mental well-being and a sense of spiritual well-being, is well established. A study at the University of Toronto found that religious conviction acts as a buffer against anxiety. Another study found that "Spiritual well-being may be cardio protective." A study at the University of Missouri found that "spiritual belief in a loving, higher power, and a positive worldview are associated with better health, consistent with psychoneuroimmunological models of health." And there are many others.

It seems that seeing the world through the lens of spiritual belief can go a long way toward promoting well-being. In other words, what you think has a profound influence on how you experience life.

So, spending time thinking about the higher, more spiritual aspects of life can enhance your experience of reality and thus your well-being. And Sanctuary is the perfect place to practice and embrace spiritual thinking. Spiritual activities that have been practiced in Sanctuary include:

Prayer – Through prayer, we experience the emotional exhilaration of union with a higher power and the sense of security and protection that union brings. We express gratitude, feel at ease with the way things are, and let go of anxieties. We pray for the people and things we need and want in our lives, forming positive affirmations that lead us to act in ways that manifest our prayers. We ask for healing, support for those who are suffering, and gain the inner peace of an open heart. We surrender our egos, our pride, and self-righteousness—along with our fears, insecurities, and anxieties—and experience mental, physical, and spiritual peace. Daily prayer can be one of the most positive habits you could adopt for a healthier and happier life.

Meditation – It is said that prayer is talking to God, and meditation is listening. The National Center for Complementary and Alternative Medicine reports that regular meditation can reduce chronic pain, anxiety, high blood pressure, high cholesterol, and the use of health care services. Mindfulness Meditation stills the mind, dissolves illusions, and allows us to see things as they really are. It works by enabling a person to have better control over brain processing of pain and emotions by teaching the practitioner to recognize, acknowledge, and let go of negative emotions without reacting to them. In Transcendental Meditation, the ordinary thinking process is "transcended" and replaced by a state of pure consciousness characterized by mental stillness, rest, stability, order, and a complete absence of boundaries. Both forms hold potential for the direct, nonverbal experience of the infinite.

Yoga – Yoga is a Sanskrit word variously translated as "connection," "performance," "application," "contact," "method," "addition," and "performance" as well as "exertion," "endeavor," "zeal," and "diligence." Sometimes described as meditation in motion, yoga helps us transcend conceptual knowledge and experience oneness with the Divine experientially. It is a physical, mental, and spiritual discipline whose goal is the liberation of the practitioner from *samsara*, the cycle of life and death. In addition to spiritual goals, yoga is also an effective exercise and physical therapy program. It is used to reduce stress and improve musculoskeletal and mental health.

Spiritual Contemplation – Spiritual contemplation is usually practiced in conjunction with the reading of scriptures, sacred texts, or other spiritually inspirational works. Bible study is one of the most common forms of spiritual contemplation. As we read and think about what we read, we begin to look at the world from the perspective the Bible presents. We begin to see life as much bigger than ourselves; we reach an understanding of our place in the universe, and realize the profound inner peace that comes from a sense of belonging.

Spiritual Journaling – You never really know what you think about something until you write it down. Then reading what you've written allows you to look at your thoughts and emotions from a whole new perspective. This is especially valuable in regard to spiritual thoughts and emotions. It allows you to express your innermost beliefs, longings and doubts, and get them out into the open where you can deal directly with them. It lets you get in touch with your feelings, off-load negative emotions, and gain clarity of mind in regard to your spiritual experience. Journaling helps you reinforce important lessons, confront important questions, and solve difficult challenges. It allows you to monitor and verify your spiritual progress. And it provides direct evidence that you are a living, growing, spiritual being.

While you journal, express gratitude. It is one of life's finest elixirs. Gratitude shifts ones focus from negative to positive, just by being grateful. It's also proven to improve physical and psychological health. First thing in the morning or at the end of the day, write five to ten things that you are grateful for.

Sanctuary provides the ideal environment for spiritual renewal and awakening on many levels.

A heart full of love
and compassion
is the main source
of inner strength, willpower,
happiness and mental tranquility.

~ Dalai Lama XIV

Chapter 7

Sanctuary Wherever You Are

Once you become accustomed to the Sanctuary lifestyle, you won't want to leave it behind when you travel. And you'll be amazed at how little it takes to completely transform a hotel room into Sanctuary. Just be sure to pack some incense or aromatic oils, small speakers that attach to your computer or other electronic device, a few candles in glass or electronic candles, and some flowing fabric to drape wherever the spirit moves you. Having all the accouterments of Sanctuary cannot benefit you if you don't actually use them. It will only take a few moments to set up your room and, when you do, you may find the fatigue and stress of travel melt away, replaced by familiar feelings of ease and comfort.

Try it. That's all it will take to convince you of its value. Take Sanctuary with you, in your bag and in your heart. Show yourself love and others will find you loveable. Live it and the whole world becomes your Sanctuary.

Six Sanctuary Samples

Here are six examples of Sanctuary spaces created by people wherever they were.

Example One – A Great Way to Start Over:

A lovely woman, who was abused by her husband, finally got the courage to leave him and rented a small apartment where she could start putting her life back together. To enhance her efforts at self growth, she painted her bedroom a soft sea foam turquoise and put in a salt lamp, waterfall, sheer flowing curtains, and a birdsong machine to transform the room into a treasured Sanctuary. Transforming this plain, simple room into her Sanctuary was easier than she had imagined and, once she began to use her Sanctuary space, her life began to improve daily. In this environment, she gained the peace of mind to begin to recognize her true beauty and self-worth and build a wonderful new life.

Example Two – Peace in the Family:

A family of five was coming apart. They were under each other's skin, especially the siblings, who argued with each other constantly. To bring peace and tranquility into their lives, they cleared out an extra bedroom that had become a catch-all room, painted it a soft teal, and created a Sanctuary space. On the outside of the door, they put up a chalk board by means of which the family members could reserve the space and all agreed it would not be used for telephone calls or video games, only as a place to pray, meditate, journal, or just to daydream! They selected comfortable couches and chairs and set up lighting in the form of a lava lamp that cast a soft blue glow over the room's atmosphere. Above the most comfortable chair, they positioned a strong light for reading and journaling. Then they put an aquarium in the room and often found themselves going in just to watch the fish and feel their blood pressures decrease. They designed their room with mindful intentions and created a Sanctuary space that was wonderfully effective.

Example Three – A Cozy Retreat:

A woman in North Dallas decided to create her own Sacred Sanctuary space in a large pantry under her stairway. This space came with its own power outlet, into which she plugged a salt lamp and a chakra color dome light. On the floor, she placed soft mattress padding and lush colorful pillows. The atmosphere she created was one of absolute tranquility comfort and coziness. Knowing that sound machines are a great help in setting a tranquil mood, she played soft music and put in a small waterfall to add to her pleasure. Under that stairway, she ingeniously created a beautiful, little Sanctuary that doubled as her Texas tornado storm shelter. She now owns three homes, each with it's own unique Sanctuary.

Example Four – Clearing the Way:

One of the key steps in creating a Sanctuary is clearing your clutter. Here's an example of how important that can be. After losing his wife to cancer, a man went into a deep depression and became a hoarder, collecting everything he could get his hands on whether he needed it or not. When he was just about to drown in all that he had collected, he had an epiphany and decided to get rid of everything. He took piles of furniture and other stuff to Good Will and immediately felt the weight of the world begin to lift from his shoulders. He found himself literally set free of all that was weighing him down and holding him back from living his fullest life. The releasing of his excess "stuff" allowed him to start a new chapter in his life. He now has a ministry helping seniors who cannot help themselves. It was heartwarming to see the transformation he made toward living a happy and fulfilled life. This is the sort of thing that can happen when we let go of the excess in our lives!

Example Five – Healer Heal Thyself:

Here's another example of just how important clearing unneeded

71

clutter can be. A wonderful healing facilitator collected everything he came across. His work area where he saw clients was a mess, yet because he was such a gifted energy worker, they all looked upon his disarray as eccentricity. Finally, his clients reached a point where they could not stand the visual chaos any longer and several of them got together and organized his mess into neat, organized categories and sections. He loved the sense of order and well-being he experienced and found a whole new comfort zone he didn't even know was possible by knowing where everything was. That's the sort of thing that can happen by following the steps in this book.

Example Six – A Total Transformation:

A lovely woman who lived in a large house on a beautiful lake wanted to turn her pool house into a Sanctuary space. After uncluttering and cleaning the space, she transformed it into a Sanctuary by painting the walls and adding new flooring and flowing curtains. She used colorful rugs to brighten and invigorate the space.

This woman also added comfortable, color-coordinated furniture, including a simple yet elegant desk and a bright modern lamp to create the perfect spot for writing her memoirs. In a western window, she hung an array of cut crystals to catch the afternoon light and break it up into rainbows that danced all over the walls and ceiling. In that dazzling wonderland, stresses often just seemed to disappear. Once it was finished, this elegant Sanctuary space became her favorite spot to pray, meditate, and daydream!

The miracle is not that we do this work,
but that we are happy to do it.

~ Mother Teresa

Chapter 8

Sanctuary as a Sacred Service

The visions and revelations I experienced during my journey to the dimension between life and death have never stopped. I receive instructions from the Holy Spirit on a daily basis telling me how to help others, how to protect myself, and how to live my life. I know what people need, person by person—one needs to be touched, one needs a better energy flow, one has blocked emotions—each one with their own individual needs. I am a conduit for the Holy Spirit and the Lord Jesus Christ. It is their love and understanding flowing through me that senses the needs of others.

For most of my life, I have hidden these gifts for fear of being laughed at or shamed. But I know God has given me a gift and that I am to share that gift with others. It's the gift of compassion, guided by a "knowing" from the Holy Spirit. It's the gift of personal Sanctuary, the gift of seeing the best in people and bringing out their inner beauty. Because of the fear, mistreatment, and isolation I have experienced, I can sense when a person needs nurturing, attention, or affection. Sometimes they just need a hug. Sometimes they need Sanctuary For Life™.

Sanctuary For Life is the non-profit organization I founded in response to my calling. It's a network of educators, leaders, doctors, scientists, researchers, humanitarians, and philanthropists dedicated to helping people take responsibility for their own well-being by integrating mind, body, and spirit. We offer educational programs for wellness, health oriented technologies, personal transformation, and spiritual growth. Through this network, our guests receive nurturing, awakening, and renewal. In a world unbalanced by stress, we help people find health and balance in their lives, discover purpose and spiritual awareness, overcome obstacles, discard old burdens, and embrace their own dynamic individuality.

Sanctuary For Life is a way of life and a vortex of inspiration, purpose, and actions that generate profound changes in personal and community life. We provide loving kindness, great awakenings, and life changing collaborations. We honor people who practice the art of compassion, people who gracefully impact humanity and those who bring healing to a world in transformation. Elegance, energetic design principles, gourmet health food, and personal nurturing all have their roles to play in our programs of rejuvenation and self-discovery.

I would not care to relive my near-death experience nor would I wish them on anyone else. Yet, I cannot deny the sense of purpose they brought me, nor regret any step along the path that has led me to where I am today. I have seen and received miracles. I have lived miracles. And, today, miracles are what Sanctuary For Life is all about. It's about miracles in health and well-being, energy and growth, personal development, and life fulfillment. It's about the transformational healing of emotional and spiritual wounds. It is part of a new world paradigm of peace, justice, and cooperation, and the embodiment of what I learned during my near-death experience.

It is what I was told to create and nurture.

Learn silence.
With the quiet serenity of a meditative mind,
listen, absorb, transcribe and transform.

~ Pythagoras

A Personal Note from the Author

Thank you for reading my book. I now invite you to put to use what you have read. When you do, you will be helping to make the world a less stressful, more peaceful, and happier place, starting with yourself. In a culture becoming more complicated, challenging, and stressful every day, creating a Sanctuary space for yourself is more important than ever. It's a space designed by you and for you as a gift you give yourself, a safe haven in a zone of tranquility where you can rest, rejuvenate and renew.

Sanctuary space enables you to meditate, pray, journal, contemplate, or just chill out and let your batteries recharge. All too often, however, because we all value compassion for others, we feel guilt or shame around doing something wonderful for ourselves. But spending time in your Sanctuary makes you a better person—less stressed, more peaceful, more sensitive—and that makes the world a better place.

So, if you should have twinges of self-indulgence guilt about feeling as good as Sanctuary can enable you to feel, I recommend that you give yourself a Passport of Permission to travel the path of a more peaceful world. In fact, I encourage you enhance the effect by including a nice cup of tea, an organic piece of fruit, or a little dark chocolate as part of your Sanctuary experience and treat your time in Sanctuary as a date you are having with yourself. Honoring thyself is a wonderful teaching.

If you share your Sanctuary with others, I urge you to set up a few ground rules for its use such as setting cell phones to airplane mode or, better yet, leave them outside of the room. Sanctuary is not a place to be disturbed by electronics, conversation, or activity. It is a place to feel blissful, peaceful, and abundant and should always be respected as such.

I also urge you to make use of the journaling pages in this book to get in the habit of putting your thoughts and feelings on paper. It's a great way to keep your intentions for your Sanctuary experience at the top of your mind and ensure their realization. As our world changes, our needs change, but we will always need Sanctuary from stress.

So, I hope you will enjoy the process of creating your Sanctuary. Have fun with it. Allow yourself to be excited at the prospect of gaining a calmer mind and a more optimistic point of view by creating for yourself a gift that keeps on giving. And when you have used your Sanctuary enough, you may find that it has taken up residence within you and become part of who you are.

About the Author

Sherri Reed

Sherri Reed is the Founder and Visionary of Sanctuary For Life (sanctuaryforlife.org), a 501(c)(3) nonprofit corporation whose mission is caring for caregivers, a mission given to her in the White Light of a near-death experience when she was seventeen. In fulfillment of that mission, Sherri operates a day Sanctuary in Dallas and two overnight Sanctuaries in pastoral settings in north central Texas where physically, mentally, and emotionally exhausted caregivers find rest, relaxation, and rejuvenation. Sherri is also a women's advocate, the host of GoodDeedAmbassadors.org, a fashion consultant, and photographer who loves showing women they are beautiful, a public speaker, and a corporate Sanctuary designer. Sherri lives in Dallas, Texas, and has a life force that lights up the lives of everyone who knows her. Her passion is helping people create their own Sanctuary spaces wherever they are.

Sherri's philosophy is simple: If you totally immerse a person in sensations proven to trigger automatic stress reduction responses in the human brain, that person will experience stress reduction. She has spent her life applying and refining this principle to the point of producing life changing experiences. *"For me, the most rewarding part of giving a guest a Sanctuary experience,"* Sherri says, *"is watching the transformation that occurs. Guests come in exhausted, drained, often depressed, and leave rested, relaxed, their spirits lifted, and feeling like themselves again."*

Sherri is known internationally as a woman who finds deep spirituality in everything and everyone she knows. She is an active member of women's celebration and support groups, and has taken a leadership role in multiple women's retreats organized around personal spiritual growth. She has the ability to sense what people need, feel their pain, and empathize with them on a spiritual and compassionate level, an ability she was given in the White Light along with her mission. Sherri has been featured in *Voyage Dallas Magazine* and the books *Unstoppable Women, Stories of American Character,* and *Glimpses into Unseen Realms.* She is a powerful ceremony leader, and a strong believer in the power of prayer and the manifestation of miracles.

Sanctuary Questionnaire

What items do you already have that you want to include in your sanctuary space?

What items will you need to gather?

What color do you find most soothing?

What will you put on the floor?

What lighting will you use to create a calming atmosphere?

What music do you have that you could use in your sanctuary?

What aromas will you use?

How will you incorporate nature into your sanctuary?

What plants would you like to have in your sanctuary?

What artwork will you use to invoke serenity?

What inspirational items will you display?

Please use the following pages to journal in.

Fill your paper with the breathings of your heart.
~ William Wordsworth

I can shake off everything as I write;
my sorrows disappear, my courage is reborn.
~ Anne Frank

In the journal I do not just express myself more openly than I could to any person; I create myself.

~ Susan Sontag

Bibliography

[1] American Psychological Association, *Stress in America – Our Health at Risk,* (2012),
http://www.apa.org/news/press/releases/stress/2011/final-2011.pdf

[2] Bruce H. Lipton, Ph.D., *The Biology of Belief,* (Hay House, Inc., 2005), p. 115-125

[3] Chan-Su Lee, Jongwoo Nam, SinWon Park, Sung Yong Chun and Ja-Soon Jang, "P1-16: The effect of visual stimuli of LED lighting by color temperature and illuminance control on attention and meditation level of mind," i-Perception (Vol 3, Issue 9, 2012)
file:///Users/jimsturdivant/Desktop/Biz/Sanctuary%20For%20Life/Creating%20Sanctuary/Research/LIGHT/i-Perception%20:%20P1-16:%20The%20effect%20of%20visual%20stimuli%20of%20LED%20lighting%20by%20color%20temperature%20and%20illumina.webarchive

[4] Menegazzi JJ, Paris P, Kersteen C, et al. A randomized controlled trial of the use of music during laceration repair. Annals of Emergency Medicine Volume 20, Issue 4, April 1991, Pages 348–350

[5] Moss VA. Music and the surgical patient. *AORN Journal* 1988; 48(1): 64–69.

[6] Kulkarni S, Johnson PC, Keatles S, Kasthuri RS. "Music during interventional radiological procedures, effect on

sedation, pain and anxiety: a randomised controlled trial," pubmed.gov 2012,

file:///Users/jimsturdivant/Desktop/Biz/Sanctuary%20For%20Life/Creating%20Sanctuary/Research/MUSIC/Music%20during%20interventional%20radiological%20procedu...%20%5BBr%20J%20Radiol.%202012%5D%20-%20PubMed%20-%20NCBI.webarchive

7 Binns-Turner PG, Wilson LL, Pryor ER, Boyd GL, Prickett CA., "Perioperative music and its effects on anxiety, hemodynamics, and pain in women undergoing mastectomy," pubmed.gov (2012),

http://www.ncbi.nlm.nih.gov/pubmed?term=Perioperative%20music%20and%20its%20effects%20on%20anxiety%2C%20hemodynamics%2C%20and%20pain%20in%20women%20undergoing%20mastectomy

8 Ulrica Nilsson, "Music and Health; How to use music in surgical care." International Academy for Design and Health, http://www.designandhealth.com/uploaded/documents/Publications/Papers/Ulrica-Nilsson-WCDH-2003.pdf

9 J Korean Acad Nurs. 2009 Jun;39(3):357-65.

[The effects of aromatherapy on stress and stress responses in adolescents].

Seo JY., Department of Nursing, Youngnam Foreign Language College, Gyeongsan, Korea.

http://www.ncbi.nlm.nih.gov/pubmed/19571632

10 J Clin Psychiatry. 2002 Jul;63(7):553-8.

Aromatherapy as a safe and effective treatment for the management of agitation in severe dementia: the results of a double-blind, placebo-controlled trial with Melissa.

Ballard CG, O'Brien JT, Reichelt K, Perry EK.

Wolfson Research Centre, Newcastle General Hospital, Institute for Ageing and Health, Newcastle upon Tyne, United Kingdom.

http://www.ncbi.nlm.nih.gov/pubmed?term=Aromatherapy%20as%20a%20safe%20and%20effective%20treatment%20for%20the%20management%20of%20agitation%20in%20severe%20dementia

[11] Am J Chin Med. 2012;40(4):845-59. doi: 10.1142/S0192415X12500632.Effect of lavender essential oil on LPS-stimulated inflammation. Huang MY, Liao MH, Wang YK, Huang YS, Wen HC. Department of Nursing, Yuanpei University, Hsinchu, Taiwan.,

http://www.ncbi.nlm.nih.gov/pubmed?term=Effect%20of%20lavender%20essential%20oil%20on%20LPS-stimulated%20inflammation

[12] J Altern Complement Med. 2012 Aug;18(8):798-804. Epub 2012 Jul 31.

Effect of sweet orange aroma on experimental anxiety in humans., Departamento de Fisiologia, Centro de Ciências Biológicas e da Saúde, Universidade Federal de Sergipe, Sergipe, Brazil.,

http://www.ncbi.nlm.nih.gov/pubmed?term=Effect%20of%20sweet%20orange%20aroma%20on%20experimental%20anxiety%20in%20humans.

[13] Complement Ther Clin Pract. 2012 Aug;18(3):164-8. doi: 10.1016/j.ctcp.2012.05.002. Epub 2012 Jun 27.

The effects of clinical aromatherapy for anxiety and depression in the high risk postpartum woman - a pilot study. Conrad P,

Adams C., Wellspring Pharmacy, Community Hospital North, Community Health Network, Indianapolis, IN 46077, USA., http://www.ncbi.nlm.nih.gov/pubmed/22789792

[14] Evidence Based Complement Alternat Med. 2005 December; 2(4): 481–488. doi: 10.1093/ecam/neh137, PMCID: PMC1297510, *A Critical Analysis of Chromotherapy and Its Scientific Evolution*, Samina T. Yousuf Azeemi* and S. Mohsin Raza
http://www.ncbi.nlm.nih.gov/pmc/articles/PMC1297510/

[15] Proceedings of the National Academy of Sciences of the United States of America, *An Ecological Valence Theory of Human Color Preference*, Stephen E. Palmer1 and Karen B. Schloss, http://www.pnas.org/content/107/19/8877.abstract

[16] W J Med Sci ISSN: 1817-3055, © International Digital Organization for Scientific Information
Online Open Access , Volume 1 Number (1) : 21-23, Jan-Jun, 2006, www.svyasadde.com/research_papers/ppe/intro.asp

[17] *Relationship Between Color and Emotion: A Study of Colege Students,* Naz Kaya, PH.D., *Assistant Professor*, HELEN H. Epps, PH.D.,
http://irtel.uni-mannheim.de/lehre/expra/artikel/Kaya_Epps_2004b.pdf

[18] J Exp Psychol Gen. 1994 Dec;123(4):394-409., *Effects of color on emotions.*, Valdez P, Mehrabian A., Department of Psychology, University of California, Los Angeles.
http://www.ncbi.nlm.nih.gov/pubmed?term=ffects%20of%20color%20on%20emotions.%20Valdez%20P%2C%20Mehrabian%20A

[19] Science Daily, *Lighting Can Influence How Wine Tastes*, http://www.sciencedaily.com/releases/2009/12/091215171510.htm

[20] Rogers S. Ulrich, Robert F. Simons, Barbara D. Losito, Evelyn Fiorito, Mark A. Miles and Michael Zelson, *Stress Recovery during Exposure to Natural And Urban Environments*, Journal of Environmental Psychology (1991) 11, 201-230, http://www.uns.ethz.ch/edu/teach/masters/ebcdm/readings/Ulrich_R_1991.pdf

[21] Roger S. Ulrich, *Natural Versus Urban Scenes - Some Psychophysiological Effects*, Environment and Behavior, http://eab.sagepub.com/content/13/5/523.short

[22] Roger S. Ulrich Craig Zimring, PhD Xuemei Zhu Jennifer DuBose, MS Hyun-Bo Seo Young-Seon Choi Xiaobo Quan Anjali Joseph, *Research Literature on Evidence-Based Healthcare Design*, Healthcare Leadership white paper series, http://www.healthdesign.org/sites/default/files/LitReviewWP_FINAL.pdf

[23] Roger S. Ulrich, PhD, *Effects of Interior Design on Wellness: Theory and Recent Scientific Research*, http://www.majorhospitalfoundation.org/pdfs/Effects%20of%20Interior%20Design%20on%20Wellness.pdf

[24] Roger S. Ulrich, PhD, *Effects of Interior Design on Wellness: Theory and Recent Scientific Research*, http://www.majorhospitalfoundation.org/pdfs/Effects%20of%20Interior%20Design%20on%20Wellness.pdf

[25] Journal for Stress Relief December 14, 201,

http://awomanshealth.com/journal-for-stress-relief/

[26] Elizabeth Scott, M.S., *The Benefits of Journaling for Stress Management*, About.com Guide
Updated May 14, 2011
http://stress.about.com/od/generaltechniques/p/profilejourn al.htm

[27] University of Mississippi research study, 2016.

[28] Drugs R D. 2017 Mar; 17(1): 53–64.- Published online 2016 Nov 25. doi: 10.1007/s40268-016-0157-5 - PMCID: PMC5318325 - PMID: 27888449 "Salvia (Sage): A Review of its Potential Cognitive-Enhancing and Protective Effects" - Adrian L. Lopresti

[29] http://pss.sagepub.com/content/20/3/385.abstract - Michael Inzlicht, Ian McGregor, Jacob B. Hirsh and Kyle Nash - *Neural Markers of Religious Conviction*

[30] http://www.ncbi.nlm.nih.gov/pubmed/21487720 - Holt-Lunstad J, Steffen PR, Sandberg J, Jensen B. - *Understanding the connection between spiritual well-being and physical health: an examination of ambulatory blood pressure, inflammation, blood lipids and fasting glucose.*

[31] http://www.ncbi.nlm.nih.gov/pubmed/20162451 - Campbell JD, Yoon DP, Johnstone B - *Determining relationships between physical health and spiritual experience, religious practices, and congregational support in a heterogeneous medical sample.*

* <u>https://www.ncbi.nlm.nih.gov/pubmed/25607117</u> - Rafer L, Austin F, Frey J, Mulvey C, Vaida S, Prozesky J. - *Effects of jazz on postoperative pain and stress in patients undergoing elective hysterectomy.*

**

<u>https://www.ncbi.nlm.nih.gov/pmc/articles/PMC1860846/</u> - <u>L Bernardi</u>, <u>C Porta</u>, and <u>P Sleight</u> - *Cardiovascular, cerebrovascular, and respiratory changes induced by different types of music in musicians and non-musicians: the importance of silence.*

***

<u>https://www.ncbi.nlm.nih.gov/pmc/articles/PMC4087081/</u> - <u>Imke Kirste</u>, <u>Zeina Nicola</u>, <u>Golo Kronenberg</u>, <u>Tara L. Walker</u>, <u>Robert C. Liu</u>, and <u>Gerd Kempermann</u> - *Is silence golden? Effects of auditory stimuli and their absence on adult hippocampal neurogenesis.*

About Sanctuary For Life

Sanctuary For Life

Sanctuary For Life is a 501(c)(3) corporation registered for educational, scientific, and charitable purposes.

Sanctuary For Life is a place of tranquility and inner peace. It is a safe haven of rejuvenation and renewal. We give back to caregivers who give generously and unconditionally to others. This includes those devoted to caring for ill or dying family members, invaluable healthcare and hospice workers who care for so many, and volunteers who give tirelessly of their time for the good of humanity. The Sanctuary For Life experience relieves stress, restores balance, and regenerates mental and emotional energy. Our guests often describe it as truly life transforming. We also teach people how to create the Sanctuary experience wherever they are. Sanctuary For Life is not just a Sanctuary. We are a lifestyle.

You are either a caregiver, know a caregiver, or one day will need a caregiver!

We invite you to visit our website and support this work, at no expense to you, by signing up to have 5% of every dollar you spend with Amazon go to Sanctuary For Life. To sign up, just go to https://smile.amazon.com/ch/91-2101321, Sanctuary For Life as your charity of choice. Thank you for supporting our efforts to give back to those who so generously live their lives giving to others.

https://www.SanctuaryForLife.org.

Products to Create Sanctuary Space

Sanctuary Living offers essentials for a healthier state of mind through products and services that help create a more peaceful and tranquil lifestyle, and a space of inspiration and serenity. The Sanctuary Living approach to stress relief immerses all the senses at once, triggering automatic stress relief reactions at the cellular level. Our mission is to reduce the amount of stress in the world and improve the quality of life. Our objective is to empower people to relieve their own stress by creating Sanctuary wherever they are.

To learn more about Sanctuary Living products, we invite you to visit our website at https://www.SanctuaryLiving.com.

CPSIA information can be obtained
at www.ICGtesting.com
Printed in the USA
FSHW020810051120
75480FS